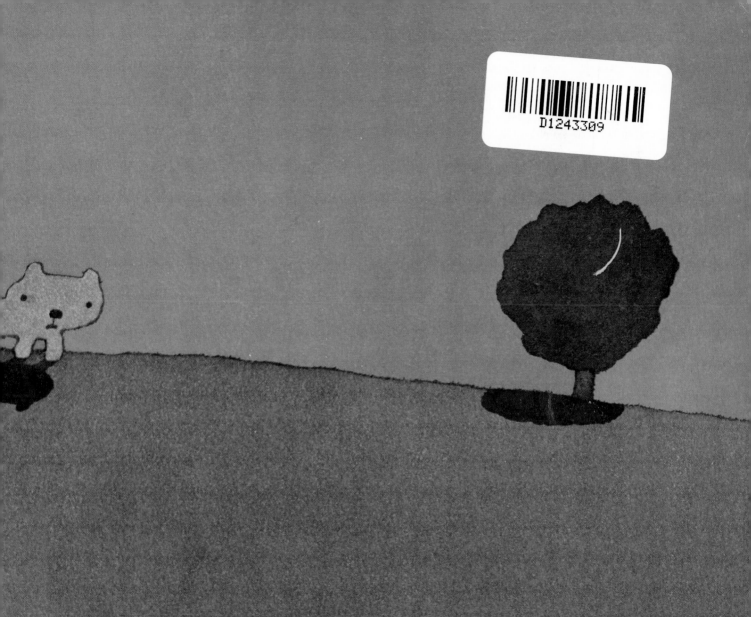

3

CATS HAVE CAT SHADOWS.

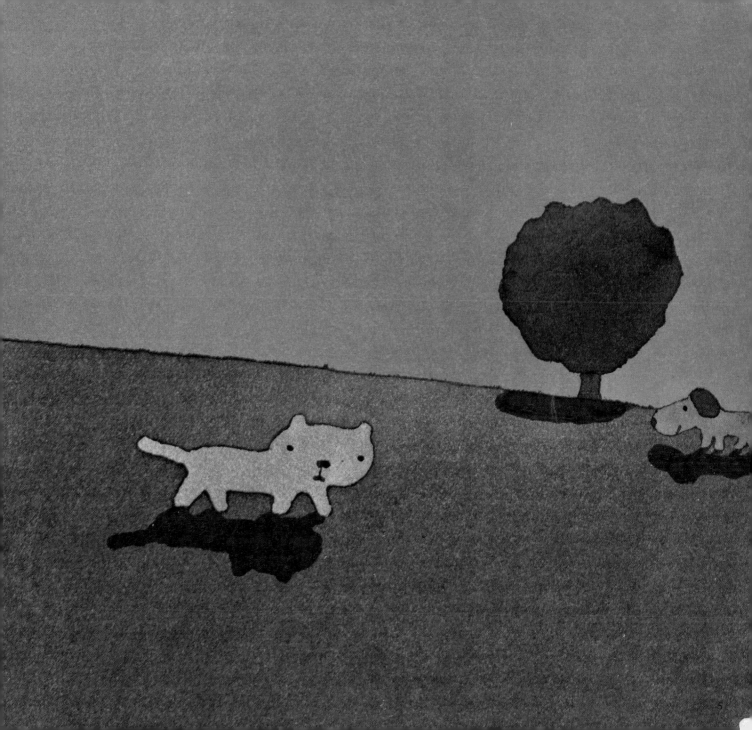

DOGS HAVE DOG SHADOWS.

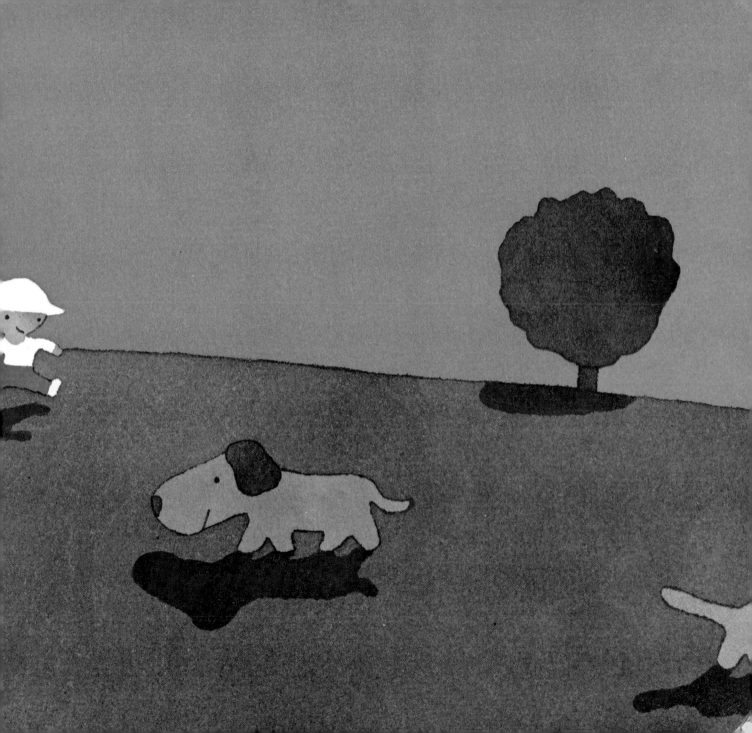

MY SHADOW CAN WALK.

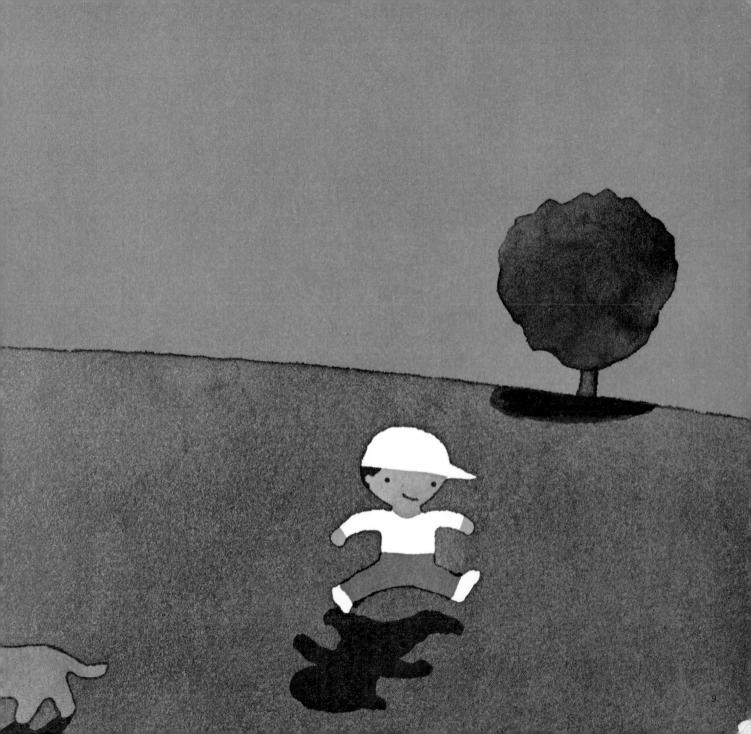

SHADOWS CAN RUN, TOO.

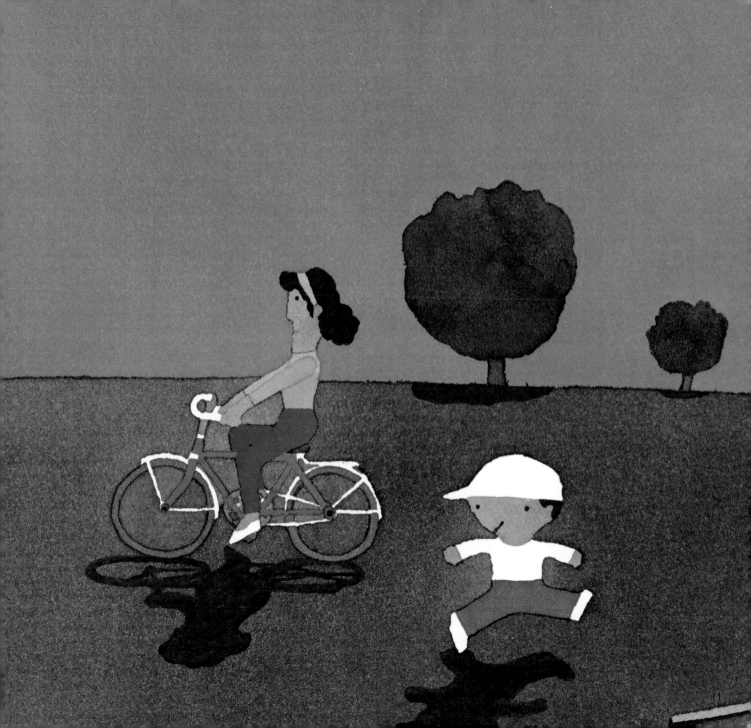

I CAN MAKE MY SHADOW BIGGER.

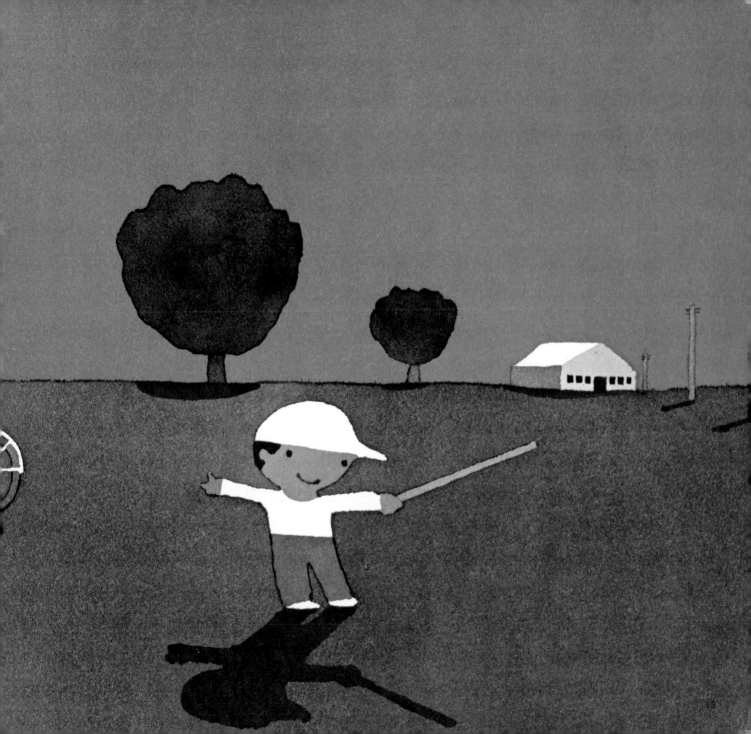

I CAN JUMP OVER SHADOWS.

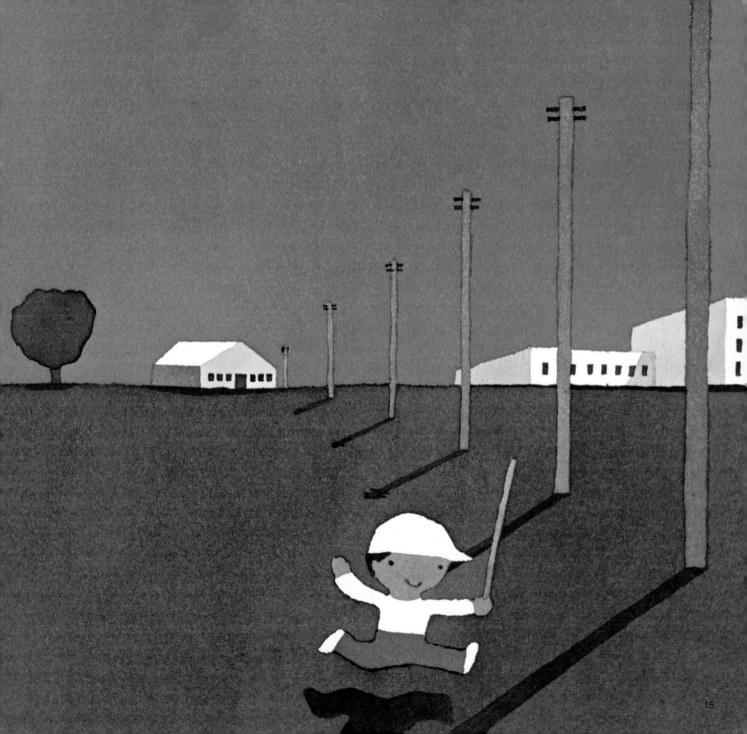

I CAN WALK INTO SHADOWS . . .

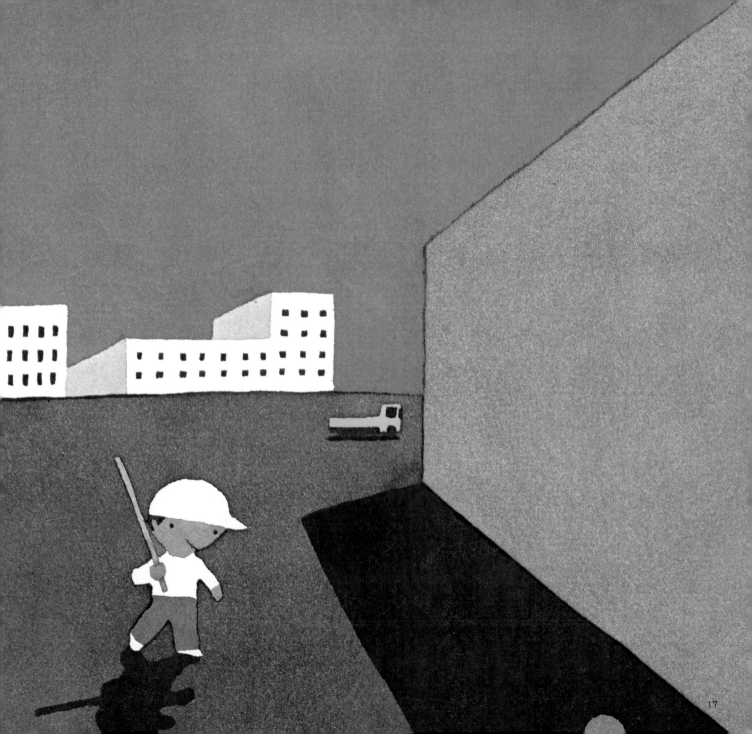

AND OUT OF SHADOWS.

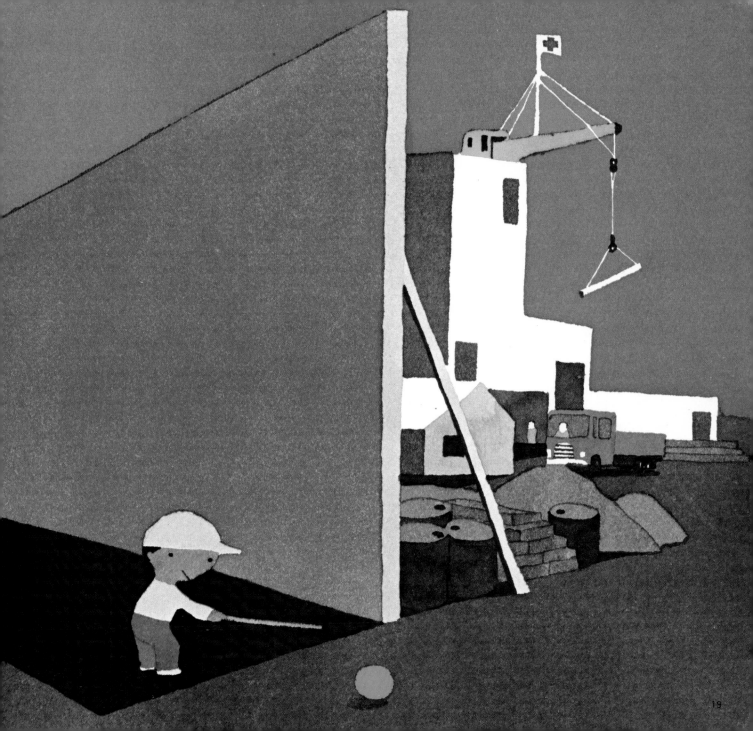

WHEN THE BALL FLIES, ITS SHADOW FLIES, TOO.

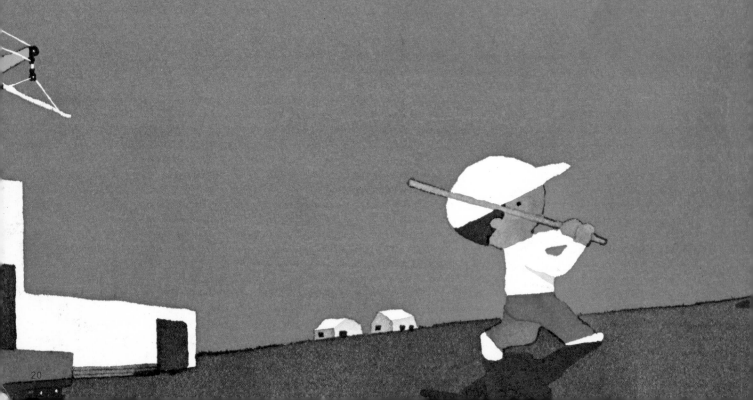

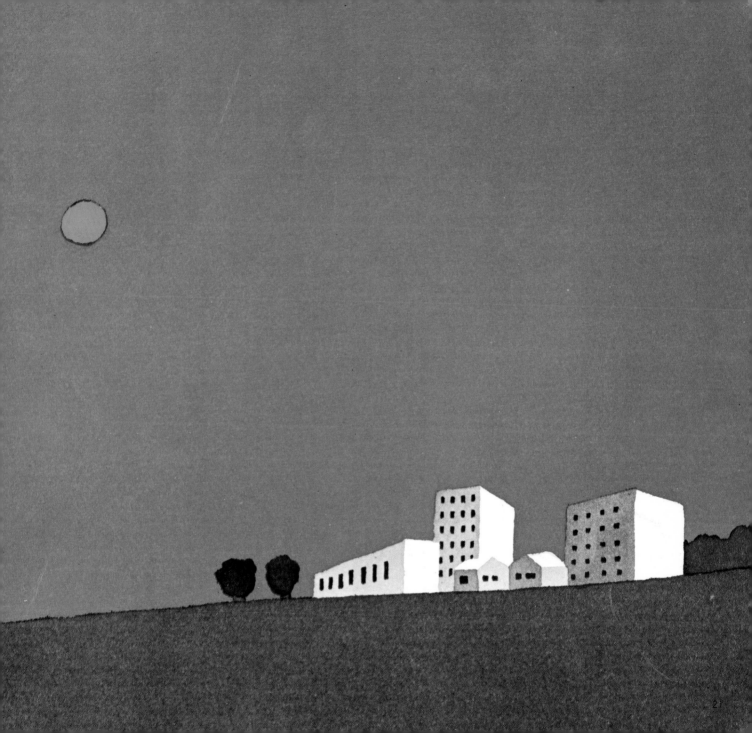

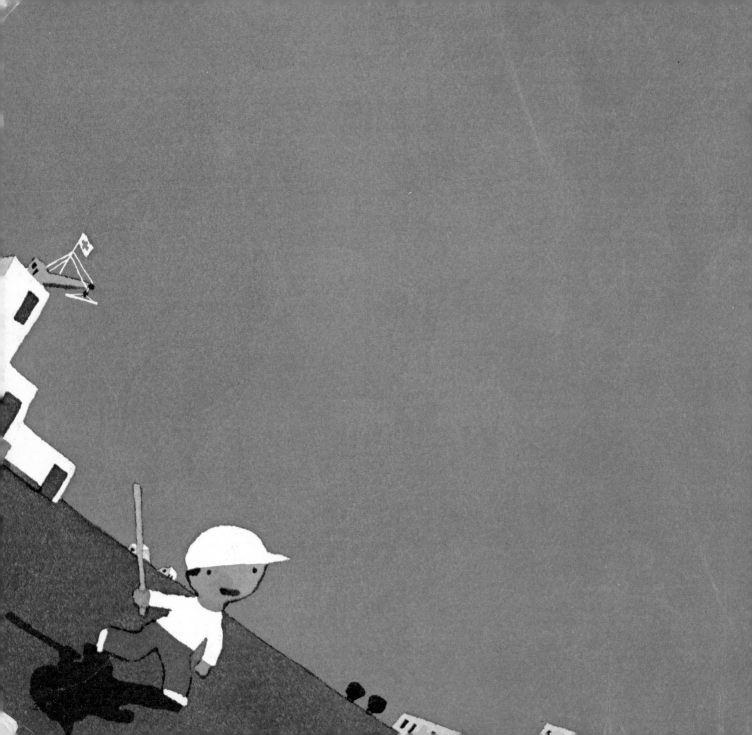